THE LION BOOK
Two-Minute
CHRISTMAS STORIES

Retold by Elena Pasquali ✦ *Illustrated by* Nicola Smee

LION
CHILDREN'S

Contents

Jesus is Born

Oh!

Long ago, in Nazareth, lived a woman named Mary. She was sitting dreaming of the day she would marry Joseph. Suddenly, an angel appeared.

"God has chosen you to be the mother of his Son," said the angel. "You will name him 'Jesus'."

"I will," said Mary.

An angel also spoke to Joseph, and he agreed to take care of Mary and her baby.

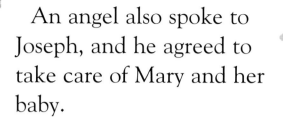

Together they went to Bethlehem.
"I'm sorry we have to go on a long journey when the baby is soon to be born," he said, "but the emperor has ordered everyone to their hometown for his people-count."

clip clop

They reached Bethlehem late in the day. To their dismay, there was no room in the inn.

"But we can make ourselves comfortable in this stable," Joseph explained to Mary.

There, where the donkey shuffled and the ox munched, Mary's baby Jesus was born.

shhhh

There were some shepherds out on the hills that night, watching over their sheep.

Suddenly an angel appeared.

"Don't be afraid," said the angel. "I have good news. God's Son has been born in Bethlehem. One day, he will rescue people from all their troubles; tonight, he is cradled in a manger in Bethlehem."

Around the messenger a host of angels sang.

Peace on earth

Then the sky went dark.

"Well," said the shepherds, "we must make our sheep safe and go!"

They hurried to Bethlehem and found the stable by the lamp that flickered within.

They found the baby wrapped in swaddling clothes and lying in a manger.

The Wise Men

THE STORY OF THE NATIVITY FROM THE GOSPEL OF MATTHEW

Look!

The men who studied the stars lived in a country far to the east.

"See that star – shining so brightly?" said one.

"I have never seen it before," said the second.

"It must surely be a sign from heaven," said the third.

They went and studied their books of lore and learning.

"The Jewish people are waiting for God to send them a great king," they all agreed.

"The star is the sign of his birth."

"We must go and find him."

They set out with rich gifts, journeying always at night so the star could be their guide. It led them over the lonely miles to the great city of the Jews: Jerusalem. Inside its walls they began asking questions. "Do you know where we can find the newborn king?"

The townsfolk were puzzled.

In his palace, King Herod was angry. "The emperor himself made me king of the Jews," he muttered.

"I will not allow a rival."

hmm

He went to consult his advisers. Then he ordered his servants to bring the men to a secret meeting. He scowled as they told him of their quest. But he had a plan.

"I can help," he said. "The holy books of the Jewish people tell of a king who is to come. God's chosen king will be born in Bethlehem.

"Go there," he whispered, "and then come and tell me where he is.

"I shall have to go and show him the respect he deserves."

The men set off. As before, the star lit the way. It led them to Bethlehem.

There they found Jesus.

"We bring our tribute to the king," they said, as they unwrapped their gifts: gold, frankincense, and myrrh.

An angel told the men not to return to Herod, for he meant to harm the child. In a dream, an angel also told Joseph to flee with his family: for Jesus was God's chosen king, and he would grow up to bring people into God's kingdom.

The Shepherd and His Pipe

A STORY FROM GREECE

tootle tootle
tootle-ee

The shepherds were gathered around a fire
on the hillside near Bethlehem.
Reuben was playing his pipe.
"Oh, do stop practising," said one of the shepherds.
"Or go further away," said another. "Quite a bit further."
"I'll go," said Reuben. "I've nearly got a new tune worked out."
"Nearly," agreed the shepherds, "but not very nearly."

Good news!

Suddenly, to their amazement, there was a flash brighter than lightning. An angel stood before them.

"Good news!" cried the angel.

"God's Son has been born in Bethlehem!

"He will be a king like no other; but now he is wrapped in swaddling clothes and lying in a manger.

"You must go and see!"

Wow

There was a moment's pause and then...

Alleluia

Alleluia

The whole sky was filled with angels – like a tree blossoming, like stars exploding.

They began singing a song with a golden tune and it seemed that heaven had come to earth.

The shepherds listened in awe. Then they whispered to one another in wonder.

"Do you recognize the melody?"

"It's the one Reuben was trying to play."

And there was Reuben, playing his pipe in tune as never before. As his notes trailed away, so did the angels' song.

"Come on, everyone," he called. "Let's go to Bethlehem and find the newborn king."

The Innkeeper's Wife

A STORY FROM IRELAND

The innkeeper's wife could be short-tempered.
   "Why didn't you just send that couple somewhere else?"
she grumbled to her husband.

   "A stable is no place to stay.

   "Well, I just hope the young woman doesn't have her baby tonight.
I haven't got a minute to spare."

   Just as the innkeeper's wife was getting ready for bed, she heard
a baby's cry. She tried not to think about it.

Bother

zzzzz...onk

Hey wa hey wa hey

Try as she might, she could not sleep. All that singing she could hear – was someone having a party?

She crept to the window; all she saw were the local shepherds cheering about something.

"Good-for-nothing lads," she muttered to herself, and she stomped back to her bed and pulled the blanket over her head.

Would nothing go right? Now the moon was shining in her window! She got up to pull the shutters tight.

To her astonishment, it was a star with a glittering tail. Some men – speaking something foreign – were pointing and smiling.

The innkeeper's wife was wide awake now. And she could no longer put off the thought she had had when she first climbed into bed.

She grabbed a warm cloak and slipped on her softest sandals before going down to the pantry.

Her husband arrived, sleepy and baffled, and she loaded him up with things to carry.

Together they went to the stable.

As they opened the door, light streamed out, and the young woman cradling a newborn baby stopped her song
and smiled.

The innkeeper's wife felt a little overawed.

"I'm sorry to have been a bit too busy to help," she said, "but I thought you might like these few things to keep body and soul together."

She and her husband laid down their gifts.

"Thank you so much," said the young woman's husband. "It's enough for everyone to share."

The Apple Tree

A STORY FROM NEW ENGLAND

Who are those strangers?

Midwinter was fast approaching, and the old man knew that he needed more firewood.

"Firewood is all that old apple tree was good for," he said to himself as he chopped.

Then, as he reached for a new log, he heard a voice.

"Is this the right way to Jerusalem?"

"It's the right way," said the old man, "but a wrong choice to go there. The king there is nothing but a villain."

"We know that a new king has been born," said a second man. "The best king the world will ever have."

"We are taking him gifts," said a third.

The old man watched them go. He chopped and chopped, and as he chopped he began to think.

"The greatest king our people have ever known was David, born in Bethlehem," he said to himself.

"Some say that one day a king even greater will be born there.

"I wonder what those strangers really knew?"

By the next morning he had
made a plan.

He went to Bethlehem with
the finest gift he could think of:
a bundle of apple wood.

Oof!

He came to a stable. Inside were a man and a woman
and a baby huddled round the glowing embers of
a fire.

The old man felt suddenly shy.
"I brought this apple wood,"
he said, pushing the sticks into
the brazier.

As the flames leaped up, the
whole room shone like gold.

"Thank you," said the mother.
"God bless you for your
kindness."

glow

When the old man returned home, what a sight greeted him. From the old stump of the apple tree, a new tree had arisen, bearing both blossom and fruit together.

The Cat in the Stable

A WORLD STORY

miaahh

When Mary's baby Jesus was born in a stable, Joseph had to find something for the baby's crib.

"The manger is the right size," he said. "If only we could chase that CAT out of it."

The cat mewed complainingly at Joseph before disappearing outdoors.

It sat and looked at the starlit world of shape and shadow.

There were shepherds and camels and a star hanging low over the stable.

It was some time before the cat crept back to see if there was room in the manger.

mew

A tiny baby boy lay there. He looked directly at the cat. The cat looked directly back; and a cat knows when it is looking at a king.

Joseph did not notice the cat.

"We must hurry," he was saying to Mary. "In my dream, an angel warned me of danger – of soldiers seeking to harm the child.

"We must go as far and fast as we can… to Egypt."

"Do you know the way?" asked Mary, gathering the child in her arms.

The cat flicked its tail. Then it ran ahead of Joseph and looked back. As Joseph led the donkey carrying his wife and child out of the stable, the cat ran further.

The same thing happened again and again. Mary was the first to notice.

Then the cat and the family became friends.

After many days, the cat and the little family arrived in a busy marketplace. It was hot and dusty. People shouted and jostled.

"Make way," came the cry, as a rich man's carriage clattered over the paving.

To Joseph's amazement, the carriage stopped.

"Miu-miu!" called the rich man to the cat. "I thought I'd lost you in Jerusalem."

My little Miu-miu

The cat leaped into Joseph's arms, and Joseph lifted Miu-miu to its owner.

"Ooh, look nice and sleek," said the wealthy man to Miu-miu. "Thank you so much for taking care of her," he said to Joseph.

"Come! Tell me your story. Let me welcome you to our town."

Mary smiled. "Perhaps its not just the angels who are looking after us," she said.

Good King Wenceslas

A STORY FROM BOHEMIA

The little page boy had had the best Christmas. There had been toys and games and a great feast. Now it was time for him to sleep in his warm feather bed with all the new and lovely things around him.

puppy

socks

slippers

sledge

He awoke as the clock struck six in the morning. He could hear his master, King Wenceslas, calling him. He hurried out of his room and joined him by the palace window.

"See that man in the moonlight?" said the king. "He's gathering firewood in the snow. Do you know who he is?"

"Oh yes," said the page, "he lives a little way off – there, where the trees start and the slope gets steep."

"We're going to visit him," said the king.

Together they went to get a big basket of food and drink from the cook.

They went to the garden and made a bundle of logs.

Then they set off.

The little page boy did his best, but the wind was buffeting him.

And the snow was deep.

whimper

splot

"Help," he squeaked.

King Wenceslas was already there picking him up.

"Tread in my footsteps," he said. "You'll find it easier."

The page boy was amazed.
Where his master walked, the
snow was gone and the first spring
flowers bloomed.

Hooray

woof

Nor did the basket seem so heavy as
together they arrived at the man's house.

The Little Juggler

A STORY FROM ITALY

red

green

yellow

As a little boy, Pietro had been part of a circus. He had
learned to turn somersaults…
to swing on the flying trapeze…

and to juggle seven balls in rainbow colours
and then add in a golden globe that shone like the sun.
The crowds clapped and laughed and cheered.

blue

indigo   *orange*

violet

Bravo

Bravissimo

As he got older, he found he was not so nimble.

"I'm really just a juggler," he told the circus.

"I can juggle with hoops

and plates

and fire

and my seven rainbow balls – not forgetting the golden globe that shines like the sun…"

Oh dear.

On the day that Pietro dropped the golden globe, the circus master asked him to leave.

Pietro started out on his own.

In the daytime, he juggled in the marketplaces. The children laughed, and their parents dropped coins in his hat.

But in the evening, he had to trudge to the next place, and in the night, he slept under the stars.

He grew old, and his limbs grew stiff.

He found himself, in the dark of winter, as a beggar outside a cathedral. It was Christmas, and people laughed as they hurried home after the midnight service.

Pietro slipped inside, hoping to enjoy the last of the warmth in the candlelit building.

All alone, he looked up at the statue of Mary and the baby Jesus.

He reached inside his bag… and began to juggle.

Higher and higher the rainbow balls flew. Then he picked the golden globe and threw it up…!

Oh

The baby Jesus had caught it in his outstretched hand, and he was sure the mother was smiling.

The Busy Baker

A STORY FROM FRANCE

The baker was busy kneading the dough.

A snowball hit his window.

He wiped his hands on a cloth and went to the door.

"Don't you get in the way of my baking," he shouted at the children.

"You'll all be wanting your fresh bread in the morning."

He slammed the door before they could even say sorry.

He finished kneading and shaped the dough into loaves.
"Now I'll just sit down a moment while the oven heats
up," he said.

He sat down in a floury old armchair
and closed his eyes.

But what was that?

giggle giggle giggle

The loaves were sitting up. They were
changing shape. They were… dough children.
"Come on, Mr Baker," they said.

whee

The dough children dashed outside and began making snowballs.

"Let's play!" they said.

And in spite of himself, the baker started making snowballs.

"Now for some fun," he said, as he tossed them at the children – dough children and real children together.

As the children dodged and darted, the baker found he was nimbler than he thought.

Suddenly the baker woke up. The kitchen door had blown open and his shoulders were cold. The oven was hot though. He slid the loaves inside.

Then he rummaged in his cupboard before measuring and mixing, making and baking.

When the families came for their Christmas bread, what a treat was in store.

"Gingerbread boys and girls for everyone!" cried the baker. "And a happy Christmas!"

Button and the Star

A STORY BY ELENA PASQUALI

Emma was walking through the park, carrying a shopping bag.

"It's a good thing we only have a small Christmas tree," she told her dog, Button, "because I only had enough money for a few decorations."

Button woofed in agreement and trotted along obediently.

Suddenly he stopped and pricked up his ears.

He gave a little growl.

Then he dashed off into the trees where it was dark and shadowy.

grrrr

"Come back, Button," said Emma. She only said it the once. A good dog needs only to be told once.

Even so, she had to wait a little before Button did come back. When he did, he had something shiny in his mouth. It was a star.

"Wow," said Emma. "It's beautiful."
The park was almost empty. Whoever had dropped the star wasn't looking for it.

"We shall take it home and put it on the tree," said Emma. "Passers-by will be able to see it in the window. Perhaps someone will recognize their lost star."

Ooh!

When Emma had finished decorating, the tree looked lovely. There were old things as well as new ones to hang, so it wasn't bare after all.

Even so, it was the star that made it very special. She and Button were sitting and admiring it when…

rat tat tat

They went to see who was knocking at the door.

"Please can I have my star?" said the angel. "It was kind of you to take care of it, but I need it for the Christmas sky."

Button growled in an angry way.

"Quiet," said Emma. A good dog needs only to be told once.

GRRRR

Emma took the star down from the tree and gave it to its rightful keeper.

The angel said "Thank you" and flew into the darkness.

Emma and Button stood watching. They both felt rather glum.

Then… a wonderful new star lit up the sky.

sparkle

It made the whole world brighter. "And look at our tree!" said Emma.

In the starlight, all the decorations, old and new, were edged with gold.